Pathways

A Journey Through Isolation

Jaque Reed

Dedication

This book is lovingly dedicated to my daughter Libby, my first born, who left us far too soon. May her lovely alto voice be added to the flights of angels who sing us all to our rest.

Except for two or three, these poems have all been written during the period of the pandemic. They are not necessarily about the pandemic itself, but were often brought out by new feelings and inner sensations that have risen during this time of uncertainty, insecurity, and dread. None of us are quite who we once were, or rather who we thought we were, but all of us have received new insights and have caught sight of new pathways opening through the thickets of doubt. It behooves us to pay attention now, to where we put our feet, and remember that turning back is not an option. Watch for the light.

Table of Contents

The Waiting House

No memories
piled up in the corners.
No dreams
spread out on the walnut table.
Somehow she seems to have left them behind.

The walls are white,
the floor, dark wood.
The windows look out on a garden
where strange flowers bloom,
without drooping, in the rain.
This is a house of waiting.

She sits patiently,
hands folded,
not quite sure why she is waiting,
or for what.
Knowing only,
that she longs for something glorious
to knock gently on the half-open door.
And steal into
her waiting heart.

Lockdown

It's not so bad,
each day a long "to do" list,
with nothing on it.
Today, however, I found myself having a conversation
with my toaster.
It went something like this:
"Why do you take so long to heat up?"
"Because I'm old and tired, dummy,
just like you."
"You're not old. I just bought you six months ago."
"Why do you think they put me on sale?"
"Didn't you notice the dust all over my box?"
"All I noticed was the ½ off sticker—
okay, go ahead, take your time."
"Thanks a bunch, I will." (sulkily)
Then out of spite,
the toaster burned my muffin.
Maybe I better find something else to talk to ...
something without an attitude ...
better stay away from the picture of my grandfather.
My coffee table and I have always gotten along well,
unless it holds me to blame for those two white rings.
On second thought,
maybe I'll just take a nap.
My bed and I have always had a very cozy relationship.
And into my dreams
drift my dearest friends.

Just For Today

Just for today,
the sun is warm
on the back of my neck.
Poppies bloom on the hillside,
nasturtiums in the valley.
Bees swarm around the old sycamore,
a lizard sits on a rock,
poised for escape,
and down by the muddy creek,
frogs are practicing their new mating calls.
Just for today,
I am content,
and just for today
it's enough.

Where Go the Goats?

The goats left us today,
not too willingly.
Herded into a truck
with the help of a black and white dog,
and a goatherd named Bill,
who wore a bright bandana around his head.
I stood at the bottom of the hill,
and watched,
a little sadly,
thinking,
"I'll miss them."
I'll especially miss Hercules,
the one who didn't fit,
who didn't match the others
in either size or disposition.
He taught them to jump higher
and clear the fence.
They all followed him in a mass of naughtiness,
to eat well-planned gardens
instead of weeds.
So, as a consequence,
Hercules was tied up outside the fence,
away from the others,
where he remained, harmless,
but bored.

I know how it feels
to be the odd one,
just a bit too different to be allowed
to mingle with the others.
The guys in charge don't like "different."
It always makes trouble.
What if the whole world ran free
what a disaster!

So as a sort of consolation prize,
I feed Hercules orange and apple slices every day.
He eats them out of my hand,
slurping them up
with his warm, soft muzzle,
and then poking his head in my purse
in search for more.
So now the goats have gone ...
No, not really gone,
just off to another dry, fire-prone hill.
Where, as an unexpected sideline,
they might just find the chance
to comfort a few more lonely souls.

So long, Hercules, my friend,
may your brave spirit remain free.
May you keep on butting your way
out of the box!
Perhaps we'll meet again
one way or another.
Maybe when I have learned
to jump over the fence too.

A Friend in Need

It is a small house
Just two main rooms,
with me and the radio.
I sometimes wander aimlessly,
looking for something to do,
something to say,
someone to say it to.
How quiet it is here.
My world is holding its breath.
Where have you all gone?

And then, into my garden,
Charlotte arrives.
(I call all spiders "Charlotte.")
Charlotte is beautiful,
large and strong and orange.
Amazingly orange.
She spins large, intricate webs
that glisten in the early morning sun,
catching dew drops, but little else.
She sits in the center waiting patiently, hopefully,
for her daily bread.
Where are all the little bugs?
Are they sheltering at home too?
I search for some to help her out,
but they are too quick, and too wary.

Charlotte perseveres.
Spins new webs every day,
trying desperately to attract a new meal.
The webs are gradually losing their geometric precision.
Lopsided, they waver in the breeze.
One end breaks loose and tears off.
Charlotte's orange is dimming.

One morning I can't find her.
Then I see her, curled up under the eaves,
wrapping all her legs around her
in a tight little ball.
She dries up quickly,
and in another day she is gone.
Gone where?
Drifting off in tiny particles,
into the universe, into the cosmos,
perhaps to recreate herself one day?

Please come back, Charlotte.
I'll still be here,
just waiting.
Or if I should not be here,
Well ... come anyway.

I Apologize

I apologize for loving the top
and ignoring the bottom and the middle.
For loving the trunk and the branches,
and not the deep nourishing roots.
I apologize for loving the rose,
and not loving the gardener.

For loving the music,
and not the musicians,
or the composer.
For loving the painting,
and not the painter.

I apologize for loving the sparkling creek,
and not its muddy, rocky bottom.
For loving the raindrops
and not the cloud that sent them down.
For loving all the early signs of spring
and not the sweet earth that brings them forth.

I apologize
for hurrying past the dark places,
the basement that houses treasures,
and the dim, mossy cave,
that hides behind the waterfall.
Have I ever said "hello"
to the sole of my shoe?

I apologize for not standing still long enough,
and for not breathing
from the depths of my lungs,
for not waiting
until the birdsong is complete.

I stand now in the vestibule of the Temple of Love,
breathing in forgiveness,
and knowing that I am ready
for a different journey
into a landscape that knows no borders
and yields only joy.
I believe some people call it Heaven.

The Last Egg

I start each day with a smile
and an egg.
The smile comes from the egg,
lightly poached,
spreading out comfortably
on a piece of whole wheat toast,
giving me permission
to spear it,
take it into my mouth,
and absorb its
sunshine goodness.
Today it was the last egg in the box.
What if it were the last egg in the world?
What if all living creatures
refused ever to lay an egg again?
Where would I be without my morning egg?
My morning smile?
Without the promise of new birth
of small wriggling beings
eager for each step forward
our world would spin slower and slower
sinking into dejection,
until we end up in the primal mud
of our own mindless beginnings.
Do you suppose,
that we,
are the last egg?

Love in the Time of Covid

If you should care,
some slightly crazy day,
to step into my heart,
you would find me without a mask,
ignoring social distancing,
and ready to give you a hug.
You would see me with all my longings,
my darkest fears,
and the tender aching of faded memories.
You might come across
an old grudge or two,
and a few pet peeves,
I'm not the perfect host.

However, we would run barefoot
down a long, green hill,
wade in a sandy-bottomed creek,
and pick white flowers
in the starlight.
We would follow a faint deer trail
along the edge of an ancient lake,
and in the splendid widening of the dark
watch stars and planets come and go.

I invite you into my heart.
Do come!
But be warned in advance,
I may just love you too much
to let you go.

Nobody's Garden

"I'm Nobody, Who are You? Are You Nobody Too?" -Emily Dickenson

I sit in a patch of late Autumn sunlight
in an odd little garden
of strange shapes and patterns
not of human design
beckoning curves from the seashore,
speckles and sharp points from the mountains,
primeval looking plants,
each creating its own natural pattern.
An ancient cow skull sulks in the corner.

It is here, in the garden of nobody,
that love is seeded, blossoms,
and begs to be turned loose.
It is here that my identity moves out,
and joins that of the wispy clouds,
becomes one with the crows
that bicker on the board fence,
and with the wet Sycamore leaves
overlapping on the wooded pathway,
with the young boy
making blissful leaps on his skateboard.

It is here, in nobody's garden
that I yield myself to the dancing forces of love,
that I am able to become
one with whatever is, was, or will be.
And am taught that to send love
into the waiting arms of the universe,
I must be willing
to become
nobody.
So please tell me,
are you nobody too?

Beach Ball

I am in tune with the waves today,
as they ebb and flow,
and spread across the sand,
in ever-changing patterns.
Each one is bearing an armload
of something delightfully familiar,
something bright, warm,
it calls my name.
It comes directly to fill an emptiness
that I have known for too long.

I play with it like a beach ball,
laughing as it changes shape and colors.
Then, on an impulse,
I toss it back on the next outgoing wave,
and watch it bob out to sea,
spreading into multicolored stripes against the horizon.

It is dangerous to hold love too closely
or for too long.
If I clutch it to me,
it will become dense as a stone,
and drop, soundless, to the earth.
So I send my gift off again,
bouncing gaily on its never-ending quest
for open hearts.

But just when I need it most,
just when I thought it would never return,
I find that it is there,
balancing lightly in my hands once again,
for love, once truly welcomed,
never really leaves.

Blackberry Man

The dawn came and went
without telling me.
No brightness streaked the sky.
No bird sang.
I awoke with tears on my cheeks,
and a dark weight on my chest.

I took my walk in the woods anyway.
My feet felt like bricks, and my heart the same.
Then I met a man with a spade,
planting blackberry bushes
all along the trail.
Soft and green and tender.
As I closed my eyes and remembered
the sweet juice of a freshly picked blackberry,
the rounded plumpness
of each shiny segment,
and the sunny trickle down my throat,
the heaviness that was trying to make a home in me
took wing, and flew away,
leaving me open to bird song once again,
to wind in the top branches,
to warm sun on my cheek.
It left me thanking our Creator
for all the small, green newness on the planet.

The one who plants blackberries
plants hope.

To the Gardeners

Everyone who loves a garden
believes in magic,
and everyone who believes in magic
loves a garden.

How can you not?
When you watch a dry, puckered seed
become the moist green shoot
silently moving towards the light,
when the small, curled bud
bursts open into a crimson rose,
when, unaided, the jasmine winds its tendrils
around the latticed fence,
when fifty sunflowers
all turn their faces to the sun,
how can you not
believe in magic?

And when the spaces around your heart
are seeded with unborn poems,
tended by gentle hands,
spring into an unexpected garden,
how can you not believe?

Blessed are they who give water
to the seeds of truth,
that they may float their own magic
into the world.
Blessed are they that tend all gardens
no matter where they may be planted,
for it is the gardeners
who find the life within death,
and send it forth
to restore lost harmonies
to an eager universe.

Land of No Regrets

We do not live there,
but only feel its vibrations now and then
just beyond the veil
of someplace else.
Not so far away,
border not even closed,
but obscured by ignorance,
and sharp spikes of ego.

It is a landscape
where the taste of a fresh picked berry
does not fade until you want it to,
nor the elusive colors of a sunset,
or the lingering warmth of a long awaited hug.
There are no mirrors.
You know you are lovely
because everyone else is.
No one calls you to dinner
because dinner is always ready,
fresh and hot.

The hills you climb
never leave you breathless,
only filled with bubbles of joy.
The loving voices you once heard
from such a distance,
are now at hand,
and you move with their rhythm.

You and I,
we long for this land,
but the solid sign at the border line,
written in the colors of the rainbow,
continues to remind us,
"not yet."

Dove Song

In her dream she stands
knee deep in meadow grass
she stops to listen
to the sweet lament
of the mourning dove
calling forth pieces of yesterday.
Gentle memories
with none of the regrets.

Paper boats float
on the creek
that used to run
to the river,
that used to run
to the sea.
Blueberry pancakes have
crisp, golden edges.
A pink silk party dress
with a lace collar
hangs, lonely, in her closet.
No place to go.

A mother's soft, warm arms,
a smile like a sunrise.
Roller skates and summer rain,
a small, drowsy head
on a pine scented pillow,
the hoot of a night owl,
whispers in the dark.
Silence.

Thus, in the summer meadow
of her old age,
the past is still alive,
and pours forth
from the throat
of a small brown bird
hiding in the leafy depths
of the cottonwood tree.

The Call

When the forest calls to you,
don't wait, go,
and go alone,
for it has something to tell you.
Stand still a moment,
and breathe the spicy pine air
singing with memories
and the richness of the loamy forest floor.

Note the fairy ring of mushrooms
underneath the oak,
the dappled patches of sunshine
on the path ahead.
Note the grey squirrel
scrabbling his way through the bracken.

Sounds of a nearby creek traveling over old stones
carrying ancient stories in its flow.
Reminders of a journey
once loved, long forgotten.
Waters never forget.
A red-tailed hawk watches you
from the top of the white pine.
In his heart he knows you,
and why you are here.
Do you?
And do you know where you are going?
And who you truly are?
Breath deeply, move slowly, with tender care,
and you will remember
what growing up taught you to forget.

No-name

Don't ask me my name today
Just for now, I choose to be
nobody.
To float like smoke
between being, and non-being.
I hear bird song,
but I will not name it,
merely travel on its silky notes
until it drifts away through the trees.
I will not name them either,
but am aware of the dappled shadows
they cast along the path.
Nor is the sweet scent of honeysuckle
any more than a dream
not yet realized.

To use words is to diminish,
to lose myself in the business of the brain.
So in this moment outside the boundaries of time,
where all creation hangs suspended in a luminous globe,
I ask again, do not ask me my name.
Allow me to sink into nobody,
just for today.

This Poem

This poem needs a haircut
and definitely a pedicure.
This poem has lived too long in isolation.
This poem has forgotten how to sing and dance.
How to caress and wipe away tears.
How to spread joy
and how to give away its heart.

The soul of this precious poem
is turning brown at the edges
like an old leaf
swept under the fence.
This poem is crying out
"Help me!"
This poem
is me.

Tulips or Ash

Today I am a tethered goat
or a pinned butterfly
fluttering its way to nowhere.
No place to go,
and even if there were,
no way to get there.
The future lies behind a porcelain wall,
too slippery to climb,
too high to peek over the top.

On the other side,
are there still cathedral bells,
and flocks of swallows writing poems
across the evening sky?
On the other side,
do swans nest on the river Avon,
and small boys still hunt for frogs
along its soft, springy banks?

Are there still sturdy barns,
and ripe fields of corn?
Tulips in the spring?

Or ...
Is it all rubble and stubble,
broken glass glittering along
streets that end too soon?
And doors that sway back and forth
on one hinge?

Is the earth parched and hardened,
sternly refusing the seed
that begs for a home?
And always, the swirling ashes?

Is there a man in a long red tie,
hiding alone
behind a pock marked pillar?

Today we shelter at home,
behind the blank wall of enigma,
each day a repeat of the last.
We wait for the drum beats of disaster
to fade away.
We wait for the windows and doorways
into tomorrow
to appear,
and wonder,
(all we have is our wondering.)
Will we find life or death?
Tulips or ashes?
Perhaps neither one nor the other,
nor even a combination of both.
But a landscape completely beyond our imagining,
into which we can step with triumph.

Memory From a Rainy Saturday

Outside, the lilacs droop lower and lower
in the spring rain,
while droplets, like tears,
slant down the windowpane.

In her special reading chair,
she sits with a dog-eared old friend
comfortably in her lap.
Dorothy, Scarecrow,
Tin Woodman and Toto
cavort across the pages,
defeating the evil Gnome King,
and gentle magic rules the day.
Good friends reunite safely,
while kindness and good cheer
restore a threatened kingdom
with a quick touch of the unexpected.

From out of the emerald-tinted stillness,
countless worlds beckon from doors
left purposely ajar,
through which the longing child
may only peek
and dream

Gratitude to the Guardians

They are still there, our splendid friends,
the trees.
In spite of all the mischief done to prevent it
they are still spreading their life-giving roots
and connecting deep into the heart of the world.
They are still reaching out to touch each other
from different sides of the road.

There is an old Sycamore stump,
bigger than my bathroom,
from which spread five full grown trees
carefully slanted, like a giant crown,
leaving each free to seek its own path skyward.
How kind they are to each other ...
so give thanks to our sturdy, steady friends,
the trees.
For long after you and I are gone,
and the planet begins to sink in despair
long after what we have known and loved has disappeared
with the last gasps of precious life,
the faithful trees will still be there
holding the shadowed planet together.
The very last thing to draw breath on this earth will be
the trees.

Child Within

There is a wild place nearby
where trees grow old and tall
without interference
their top branches blending,
their root systems entwined,
the forest floor in comfortable disorder.
Through it a small muddy creek
plods its way to the sea.

It is here I bring my child within
when the snarling dogs of politics,
the purple, red, and oranges of the plague
cause her to whimper
and cry out for help.
As once, so long ago,
she guided me deep into another forest
far older, far grander,
and taught me to dance.

So we travel again to the trees
where they will sing her soft green lullabies
and bid her to remember kinder days.
I wrap my arms around her
to keep her safe
even though,
so far as the eye of the heart can see
there is no safe.

Whose Lettuce?

"It's not yours, it's mine!"
"Who says so? What's underneath belongs to me!"
"Well, I planted it,
I watered it,
I watched it grow,
and now it's ready for MY salad!"

"But I watched it too
from my dark, sleepy tunnel,
and waited for it to be ready,
and now I want it for MY salad!"

And so we tug,
in the cool, dewy morning
one from the bottom
and one from the top,
each determined
to win the battle
of "whose is it?"

At last, the lettuce,
accepting the inevitable,
snaps in two.
The invisible gopher
scrabbling off with his half,
and I, left with a handful of crushed leaves—
hardly enough for a salad.

Somehow, I find myself hoping
that somehow,
my determined little adversary
has ended up with enough ...
Isn't enough all we need?
All that we should ever ask?

Holy Saturday

Today I cried for Jesus, cold and alone
in his dark tomb.
No one to sit Shiva with him.
What was really going on in there, anyway?
Were a host of gentle angels
restoring his body for its quiet return?
If so, they left the wounds in his hands—
no prettying him up.
And why did Mary, who knew him so well
mistake him for the gardener?
Why was she not allowed to hug him?
Would it upset a not yet completed
balance between flesh and spirit?

So many questions without answers.
So many tears with
no one to dry them.
Through it all,
I know only one thing.
That tears are not enough.
They are only the beginning
of a long and loving journey.

Mosaic

I am from nowhere, or perhaps everywhere.
I am from a meadow deep in a forest, from a rock formed
before time existed.
I am from the wind and the rain, and wild strawberries.
My home is in a forest
that fought its way back from desolation.
I am from a mossy bed
between two white pines,
where in an altered state,
I view an altered world.
I am from a grandmother with a wobbly chin,
from a stubborn old man who taught me
how to fold flags and splice rope.
From a melancholy father who took his own life,
and a mother who never stopped blaming herself.
I am from a stowaway and a sailing ship,
fleeing a revolution.
I am from a doctor who shook his cane at a man of God,
and damned him to Hell.
I am from moments of listening to grass growing,
and weeping over the body of a dead rabbit.
I am from an old clock with broken hands,
that goes on ticking anyway.

I am from all these things,
but much more:
I am from the first primordial mudpuppy
that dragged itself onto dry land,
and so are you.
This is how you and I become We,
and it is We who will keep the heart of our planet beating,
not you and not me,
but We.

Dream Catchers

Dreams are our inner story tellers,
where we learn,
like Alice,
that to get where we are going,
we have to reverse ourselves.
We learn that
life is not what it seems,
nor are we quite
who we thought we were,
that when the sun is setting,
somewhere else it is rising.
We learn the music is made of colors,
and that we are nourished with the light
that throbs
in a closely woven fugue.

We move in a wedge of wild geese,
each guided by the same
sweetly murmuring voice
telling us when to lead,
and when to fall back.
Time and space
are unknown in dreams.

Terrors, clawing at us
from the wide-awake world,
interrupt the peace of infinity,
drag us back to a landscape of doubts,
and disillusions,
to a place that is not
our true home.

Only a fragment of us is born in the Now,
but that fragment still clings fiercely
to the muddy half-truths
and odd distortions
we have always cherished.

This is what our dreams attempt to show us,
but we wake
and we forget,
and are separate once again,
each on our own patch of sand,
having shaken loose from the mighty cosmic wave
in which our hearts were born.

Some day we shall be gently wrapped
in a dream from which we shall not wake,
and we shall be free
to follow our storytellers
to where all rivers join,
and all pathways merge
with the one.
And we shall greet our true selves with joy
thus a new story will be born,
and we learn even deeper truths,
from our kindly catchers of the dream.

What's Missing Here?

Legions of governments
make the rules
they swear by them,
we live by them,
but nothing changes.
The planet goes its own way
grimly laughing at us.
Plagues, earthquakes, floods,
famine, wild fires and drought,
and we still don't get it.
We still argue bitterly,
and kick each other in the shins.
Deny, deny, deny,
and smash some windows
while you're at it.
Sneer, name call, sow distrust
and fear.

Above all, never trust.
Not even in God—
especially in God.
Where have all the smiles gone?
and hands that reach out
past the man-made boundaries?
Black ants, scurrying through the dust
show more purpose than we.

Someone, please, bring back our joy,
and all the halleluiah songs.
Love is escaping through the back door.
Someone, please, reach out,
further than you ever thought you could,
to haul it back in again.
To cradle it safely
in our crumpled hearts,
and set our feet upon a path
that leads to truth.
Making sure that we pick
the wildflowers along the way.
They are meant for us,
for in the small, fragrant beginnings
that grow close to the earth,
we will always find
the newest, and truest
reasons for hope.

Gathering In

Shadows on the wall
whispers in the wind,
drifting shapes—
memories.

Moonlight casts a long shimmering path
across the dark water.
Paddles dip silently
shedding gleaming silver drops.
A sharp scent of evergreen
floats along the night air.
Children's voices (mine as well),
wild in the last games of the evening.
Loon calls.

The clang of a trolley bell,
mounds of grimy snow
melting in the alleys,
liquorice whips, and marshmallow bananas,
cold, gritty wind—
winter in the city.

Massachusetts hillsides
greening up in April.
A young woman, standing at the window watching,
arms full of folded sheets.
A tall, slim boy-man
sneaks up behind her,
and feathers a soft kiss
on the back of her neck.
Joy unfurls like a peacock's tail.

A car crash,
a dim, dream-like funeral,
and all is over,
or so it seems.

New love,
new life,
new memories.
Children spun out of sunshine,
sweet lullabies at bedtime.
The penny candy shop is gone now,
peanut butter cups are the new candy king.
The smell of rain
on hot summer sidewalks,
a small, gummy hand in mine.
The swish of silk around my ankles
in a long, lingering waltz.
Champagne bubbles
shine through candlelight.

The sun rising over the dome of St. Peter's,
the hum and buzz of Vespas beginning their day,
a fishpond with sides covered in ivy.
I can't quite reach to see in.
The scent of brewing coffee everywhere.

Where do the memories go
when I join that wedge of wild geese
on their way to another home?
May I bring them with me
in a carry-on bag?

Or do they rest behind in their own small grave?
I shall be on my way to make new memories now,
but the old are so precious ...
might I tuck a few of the sweetest
in a back pocket somewhere?
Only the most dear, the most fragile,
the ones who would not survive if left behind
in the dust of another time.
No one would visit them,
and their tiny moments of glory
would be forgotten.
Even by me.

Reconciliation

She was so young and so curious,
as we all are, over the hidden and the mysterious.
So she opened the box.
Poor Pandora!
Out flew swarms of vicious, stinging insects
intent on maiming and destroying the world.
But as she lay fainting, and half dead,
something stirred and shifted,
and a luminous white butterfly
fluttered out of the depths,
and kissed her.
Then flew off to heal the wounded world.
Strange—
it takes millions to wound and murder,
but only one butterfly named Hope,
to comfort and to heal.

Grace

Every now and then
and by grace alone,
I am allowed to dip my cup
into the ancient well of wisdom,
and sip its cool, sparkling waters
that allow the eyes of my spirit
to open wide and perceive
mysteries from the past
that bring new meaning
to today and tomorrow.
But if I should ever claim
this blessed water as my own creation,
its insights drawn from my own heart,
then by the same grace,
the privilege will be withdrawn.

No Pot of Gold

You must be up
very high indeed,
to see that
a rainbow has no end,
that it is
a smooth circle
of inconstancy.
No color is ever perfectly itself,
for just when it seems to be
most purely original,
it has taken on another tone.
Yellow does not turn suddenly
into orange,
but blends softly
until the two
become one.
The blue you hold so dear
has blurred and merged,
into another splendour
equally beloved.
You cannot hold onto that luminous green,
that is slipping past itself.
Would that you could catch
the bonbon pink
and touch it to your lips!
But it has drifted off into otherness.

You will never hold back
the magnificent becoming
of a rainbow.

We think we are standing still,
but we are not.
We think we see the rainbow as it is,
but we do not.
We think our lives are real,
but are they?

Only change is real.
Only change never changes,
and we are never who we think we are.
We are only becoming,
and how glorious a dance it is!

Solomon's Reminder

The small, muddy creek
moves slowly toward the sea.
In the tangled islands
of twigs and dry leaves, are knotted
the debris of countless memories,
the disillusion of abandoned dreams,
and prayers with chewed, ragged edges.
All float in the same direction,
to the sea.
In time,
these discarded fragments of yesterday
are lifted up to be purified
and reawakened
in the radiance of the sun.
Clothed again in hope,
they pour down in a cloudburst of love,
moistening the earth,
and plumping the eager seeds with promise.

Thus we are called upon to remember
the words of an ancient king,
"There is no new thing under the sun."

Our plague-weary world
smiles,
and prepares
to begin again.

Word Basket

Words are like silken ribbons
slipping through my fingers.
I catch them all in my green and yellow basket.

The daring impermanence of a snowflake,
the surprise of a barn owl with a backward head,
the yin and yang of the tidal flow,
the mystic greening of the forest,
the filigreed shadow of a bare branch
casting its immortal shadow across the path.
New ducklings of hope float beside
the ancient bogs of misperception,
a muddle of mud clogging my dreams,
the rusty trickle of memories,
the looping river of consciousness
churning up the grim growl of the future,
the whirling dervish dust motes
in a slanting ray of morning sun.

I carry all these in a basket
woven of glory and gloom,
while gentle light from another landscape
filters through the frazzled chinks.

The Seeker

The bright plaid
of a small girl's hair ribbon
is echoed
in her ache for adventure.
Born to wander,
she roams in all directions
searching for an escape hole
in the fabric of the Earth.
She knows they are there waiting
for her sudden discovery,
but the clever mysteries,
the hidden gaps,
remain concealed
in the tangled density of the planet,
giving forth their mystic vibrations
in faint, sweet songs.

Oh, where is the source
of the yellow brick road,
the door in the back of the closet?
Behind what horizon
lies the wrinkle in time?

Travel on, little girl,
and pay attention on your way.
Learn to dwell in tiny spaces,
and love the wings of a beetle.
Scoop up the hum of the universe,
and make it your own.

There will be some fine and glorious day
of discovery.
But in the meantime, little wanderer,
always remember
be home
in time for dinner.

Combo of Memories

Yesterday I sat outdoors and listened
to a Yamaha piano
and a beautifully contoured bass
play soft jazz tunes from the '40s and '50s
"Lullaby of Birdland,"
"These Foolish Things,"
"Emmaline,"
"The Shadow of Your Smile"
and so many others.
All part of another note-filled life.
Nostalgia hit me like a runaway truck,
knocking my memory bank to pieces,
I could smell the grit
and the exhaust
of the Chicago night air.
Feel the beat and hear the joy filled tones
coming from the open doors
of the many cafés and bars
that surged to life along Rush Street.
I sat again in the dim lights of the "Blue Note"
wrapped in the voices of Ella, and Sarah,
the horns of Dizzy and Lionel.
I felt the delight of a first love,
and a warm hand covering mine.
A few tears sneaked out of my eyes,
and were soaked up
by my tired old Covid mask.

Yesterday is an illusion.
The sweetest of memories
rest in the tender spaces around our hearts—
the places that do not recognize time.

Memories are patient,
simply awaiting their chance
to escape into the raw space we call "today"
and shake loose our tears
as well as our smiles.

Unwelcome Guest
Based on "The Guest House," by Rumi

The doorbell rings with unpleasant urgency.
Oh dear, it's Uncle Dreadful ...
Again!
There he lurks,
with his stubbly chin,
and his dirty fingernails.
He carries a scruffy briefcase
filled with packets
of doom and gloom.
Dust motes of misery
float around his head.

Go away, old man!
I have enough lopsided visitors
in my parlour.
No room for you now.
You need a long, hot shower,
outside and in.
Come back when your hands are clean,
and there is a smile on your face.
Instead of a smirk.
Come back when your shadow
is not long and murky
and radiating fear.
Then maybe I will let you in ...
or maybe not.

Midnight Mirror

Did you ever look in a mirror
and see someone else?
I don't mean someone else beside you,
I mean only someone else.

Last night,
when I made my usual pilgrimage to the bathroom,
I glanced in the mirror and saw
a magician pulling red scarves
out of his sleeve.
He winked at me,
and turned into a white haired-woman
playing solitaire,
slapping the cards down
as if in some sort of punishment.
She faded off and became
a small boy
wandering in the woods.
I think he was crying.
The boy faded away
and became a group of brown and white rabbits
huddled under a tree,
watched by a hungry hawk.
Suddenly the rabbits were six children
all pointing long, accusing fingers
straight in my startled face ...

This last was too much for me,
so I staggered back to bed.
But when I turned back the covers,
I found I was already there.

Seraphinite

Smooth, oval stone,
the color of a leaf,
harbors a forest
of pearl white angels
with warm
softly feathered wings,
awaiting their call
to enfold the world
in love.

Changes

If I could change the color of my eyes,
would anyone notice?
Would anyone care?
If I could change the direction of the morning breeze,
what difference would it make?
If I could persuade an apple tree
to turn its fruit from green to red,
how would it affect the planet?
But if I could change the breadth and depth of my heart,
show it how to slip past its self-satisfied boundaries,
if I could thaw the cold spots,
and teach it to sing a sweeter song,
then maybe, just maybe, it would reach,
down to the core of the world
and teach it a new song as well,
and remind it of the joyful dance
it left behind so long ago.

Nightmare

Last night I escaped
across a floor littered
with shards of broken glass.

I drove in an old car
down a dark forest road.
Headlights wouldn't work,
couldn't stop,
drove blind
into a stubbled meadow
that held a cottage
that looked like mine,
only the key wouldn't turn.

A sense of doom
coming up from behind,
and I jumped
into a shallow river
swarming with snakes.
One of them
curled itself around my leg.

With a sudden gasp
I awoke,
and left the demons behind
squirming in their own dark realm.
Outside my window the sky was turning blue,
and clouds
like little pink boats,
floated serenely westward.
A flock of small birds
sang to each other
as they headed toward the sea.
I put my hand on my heart,
to call its frightened fragments together,
and smiled at the vanished terror.

Now, as I sit with my coffee,
I begin to wonder
which is dream
and which is real?
Mercury in retrograde?
No, I am in retrograde.

Up

When you find your staircase,
the one that leads to a star,
don't look back,
don't look ahead,
don't look up,
don't look down,
just keep climbing.

Who Are You?

You are not
who you were yesterday.
You are not
who you will be tomorrow.
You are only
who you are today.
Be gentle with that self.
Love, like the petal of a rose,
bruises easily.

Incomplete

Love,
without joy,
is a river
that has lost
its luster
in the steaming heat
of the sun.

Love,
without tenderness,
is a child
left alone
in a dark room.

Love,
without understanding,
is an empty beggar's bowl
tipped by the side
of a dusty road.

Love,
without a smile,
without a song,
without a dream,
is dead.

The Passenger

I love train rides.
It's on its way
like a slow freight
lumbering down the track.
No crossing bell rings out yet
and the gate has not come down,
but I can feel the faint vibrations
humming along the rails.
I have been clutching my ticket
for a long time.

I hope I can ride in the caboose,
and watch the scenery of the past
slide on by.
There might be places where I am tempted
to hop off and linger for a while ...
A village with a gazebo
and a July 4th parade,
a city where countless deep bells
ring out at dusk,
stirring up clouds of swallows.
Where priests buzz by on their Vespas,
and wimpled nuns cram into tiny Fiats.
There might be a lake at the edge of a wood
where loons signal each other
across dark waters,
and new balsam scents the evening ...

But no, they will quickly spin out of sight
without a trace.
They are only memories,
just tapes, not meant to be played again.

This will be a journey
to the mysterious "someplace else,"
a landscape that has beckoned
in many long ago dreams.
With sweet and tempting song.
A place of new wonders and adventures,
a place of love and compassion.
I have no return ticket,
and the tracks disappear behind me.
An Emerald City rises ahead,
singing softly in the mist.
Oh yes, I love train rides!

Tuning Fork

"Do you know,"
asked the angel,
"That you have always existed?"
Not in your personhood,
but in your soul.
You have circled the universe
as the clear vibration of a tuning fork,
the last deep note of a cello,
the sweet lament of a mourning dove.
You have echoed in the howl of the alpha wolf
calling the pack together
as winter storms approach.

You have drifted in and out
of every color that exists on the planet,
and some that do not.
You have glided like a dry leaf
along all the great rivers of the world,
and have drifted up every snow-capped mountain
that has raised its head above the clouds.

You have been a droplet in the waves
that crash upon the continental shores,
and a bubble in the sea foam
that spreads across the sand.
You have watched kingdoms come and go.

You have been sweetness
in a field of summer clover,
and the juice in a wild strawberry
drooping lower in the rain.

You are complete.
And so are all the wanderers,
those who search out truth.
I come to tell you this:
Trudge the world no longer,
seeking the Balm of Gilead,
for it lodges in the palms of your hands,
and sparks forth from your fingertips.
Stand still in your own garden,
and give glory to God!"

Reunion with Life

The door is open once again,
and through it slides ripples of love,
coaxing us to venture out once more,
out into a treacherous world,
out into a world that once chased us in,
made us fearful of touch,
and the softness of a loved one's skin.
Put love at arms length.
And the lack of it
troubled our dreams.
Now feathered voices are calling us forth,
waking us to new pathways,
new dreams.
But sharp prickles of awakening
hold us wavering on the threshold.
(Something in us
really wants to go back to bed.)
But the beckoning angels sing on,
reminding us that
no one ever became a saint
by hiding behind a closed door.

I Am Not

I am not my brain
that figures and configures,
and sends me down monkey paths
of misunderstandings.
I am not my heart
that bravely pumps blood
day after day,
moment after moment,
into my waiting veins,
and sends love notes
out into the world.
I am not my tongue
that is prone to tripping
over the pebbles
of everyday conversation.
I am not my skin, or my flesh,
or my bones.
That is only where I live.
Most of all, I am not my fears
that chase each other like squirrels,
and pinch me awake at midnight.

If you will gently brush away
all that I am not,
then there I shall be,
happy and shining and free,
just waiting for someone like you
to find me.

A Walk in the Park

Down from the nearest tree
spun a leaf
that landed with a flourish
just at my feet.
I stopped and marveled
at its fiery red,
and filigree
of golden veins.
When I looked up,
a woman on a bench
gave me a smile
so filled with love and compassion
that I put it in my pocket
to keep out the chill,
and walked on.
Then I saw a ragged old man
feeding peanuts to the squirrels,
and eating half himself,
so I gave him the smile,
and he smiled back.
Mist in his eyes—
mine too.
When a little boy fell down,
and skinned his knee,
I gave him the old man's smile,
and he gave me a sheepish grin
and limped back to his mother.

I passed the grin on
as I unwound a tangled dog leash
from the frail leg of an elderly woman.

The smile she gave me in exchange,
was so sweetly grateful
that I decided to keep it for myself.
I needed gratitude that day.
Gratitude to the universe,
gratitude to God,
gratitude to a red leaf
that fell, not without purpose,
directly onto my path
on a day of disillusion.

Gifting

One day when your spirit feels light as air,
gather your freshest, greenest dreams in a basket,
and go a-scattering.
Toss some in a meadow
sparkling with daisies,
some under the old wooden bridge
that crosses the creek,
some in a ditch by the road through town,
some by the steps of your favorite haunted house.
Scatter wherever the ground looks needy.
They will take root,
they will sprout,
they will come into bloom.
Some soft spring day
a small boy on his way home from school
will pick a bunch for his mother,
and on her wobbly kitchen table
they will sing to her.
An old man with a cane made of sturdy English Ash
will press a blue posey in a book of poems.
A year later his granddaughter will find it,
and hold it against her heart.
A rabbit snatches a yellow blossom
just before the hawk pounces.
Ah, don't cry,
he holds his ticket to another life
safe between his teeth.

So give with abandon.
Our dreams do not belong only to us.
Dreaming is how we gift the world
with the most tender fragments of our soul.
Dreams are the sweet breath of the universe.
They are only on loan to us.

Hidden Waters

When the well-planned parks
shrivel and crumble,
when the royal gardens
have gone to seed,
meadows will still bloom
in random splashes of glory.
New green shoots will burst through
the slowly widening cracks
in neglected pavement,
and hidden waters will still reflect
low-hanging branches
of woodland birch.
And serpentine rock
embedded in the mountainside
will feel free to share
its paleolithic secrets.

As the garden gate,
with its broken hinge, swings back and forth
with a rusty creak of despair,
it is the climbing nasturtium
that will weave sturdy tendrils
around and through corruption,
bringing forth a new song.

It is unshod feet
that will create new pathways
into the landscape of hope,
and at the very end,
it is the wild
that will win.

The Bears—

In Memory of the Montecito Mudslide

One dark, rain-soaked night,
a mighty bear
stood on its hind legs
and bellowed.
In reply,
the hills shivered
and let go
with a series of deadly moans,
dragging all in their path
to a shuddering, choking death.

The sun rose in the morning
and shone through the broken windows
of shattered homes,
and shattered lives.

Long anxious months later,
we thought hope had won the day,
when bridges were built once more
over the distorted creek beds,
and traffic moved smoothly
across streets once seeming beyond repair.
Nasturtiums began to bloom
on the barren piles of debris.
Not so simple—

All over the planet,
other bears have risen up,
heralding with hoarse, echoing voices.
Fire, storm, warfare, famine and plague.

How many more bears are there,
waiting in the forest
for their turn to announce destruction?
How many more chances will there be
for wildflowers to bloom again
on mountains of human pride?
We have forgotten how to listen.

Not So

The crows outside my window
all call, "gone, gone, gone."
As I turn the pages of my book,
the words slide off
and onto the floor.
When I pick them up,
they all say, "gone, gone, gone."
And off they go,
echoing down a long canyon of grief.

The words do not tell the truth.
You will never be gone.
You are in the pulsing flicker of the farthest star,
the soft hoot of a barn owl,
the juice of a wild spring strawberry,
the smile of the kindest friend,
and the first cry of a newborn baby.
You are there each day,
when I open my eyes,
and at night
when the dark settles
across a reluctant sky.
You are shadows,
you are sunlight,
you are rain
winding through the treetops.
You are my first born,
and I feel your fetal heartbeat
flutter against my breast.

The words are a lie.
In the mysterious magnificent cycles
of this universe,
where creation and destruction
move in tandem,
there is no such word as "gone."

Being Ninety

Some days I feel am going to die tomorrow.
Some days I feel I am going to live forever.
Some days I WANT to die tomorrow.
Some days I want to live forever.
Good thing it isn't up to me.

CPSIA information can be obtained
at www.ICGtesting.com
Printed in the USA
BVHW021201280322
632575BV00018B/332